COOL CATS

Siberians

by Betsy Rathburn

BLASTOFF!
2
READERS

BELLWETHER MEDIA • MINNEAPOLIS, MN

Note to Librarians, Teachers, and Parents:

Blastoff! Readers are carefully developed by literacy experts and combine standards-based content with developmentally appropriate text.

Level 1 provides the most support through repetition of high-frequency words, light text, predictable sentence patterns, and strong visual support.

Level 2 offers early readers a bit more challenge through varied simple sentences, increased text load, and less repetition of high-frequency words.

Level 3 advances early-fluent readers toward fluency through increased text and concept load, less reliance on visuals, longer sentences, and more literary language.

Level 4 builds reading stamina by providing more text per page, increased use of punctuation, greater variation in sentence patterns, and increasingly challenging vocabulary.

Level 5 encourages children to move from "learning to read" to "reading to learn" by providing even more text, varied writing styles, and less familiar topics.

Whichever book is right for your reader, Blastoff! Readers are the perfect books to build confidence and encourage a love of reading that will last a lifetime!

This edition first published in 2018 by Bellwether Media, Inc.

No part of this publication may be reproduced in whole or in part without written permission of the publisher. For information regarding permission, write to Bellwether Media, Inc., Attention: Permissions Department, 5357 Penn Avenue South, Minneapolis, MN 55419.

Library of Congress Cataloging-in-Publication Data

LC record for Siberians available at https://lccn.loc.gov/2016052716

Text copyright © 2018 by Bellwether Media, Inc. BLASTOFF! READERS and associated logos are trademarks and/or registered trademarks of Bellwether Media, Inc. SCHOLASTIC, CHILDREN'S PRESS, and associated logos are trademarks and/or registered trademarks of Scholastic Inc.

Editor: Nathan Sommer   Designer: Lois Stanfield

Printed in the United States of America, North Mankato, MN.

Table of Contents

What Are Siberians?

Siberians are fluffy cats known for their thick fur.

Three heavy **coats** cover their round bodies. The coats keep them warm and dry.

Siberians love to be around people and other pets. They see them as playmates.

Sometimes these cats splash in water for fun!

Siberia, Russia

Siberian cats come from a cold part of Russia called Siberia.

There, the cats were used as **mousers**. Their thick coats kept them warm as they hunted.

Elizabeth Terrell was the first American **breeder** of Siberians. She received three Siberian kittens from Russia in 1990.

Americans soon
fell in love with this
charming **breed**!

Large and Colorful

Siberians have large bodies and strong legs. Longer back legs help them jump and climb.

tufts

Siberian paws are big and round. Some have **tufts** of fur between their toes!

13

ruff

These cats have **bushy** tails.
They wrap their tails around
their bodies to help stay warm.
Ruffs of fur circle their necks.

Siberian Profile

thick ruff

round body

bushy tail

Weight: 8 to 25 pounds (4 to 11 kilograms)

Life Span: 11 to 15 years

Siberians have semi-long hair.
It can be any color or pattern.

Siberian Coats

tortoiseshell

tabby

point

solid

Tortoiseshell and **tabby** are common patterns. Some Siberians have **point coats**.

Acrobat Cats

Siberians are fearless cats. They jump high for toys and treats.

They often flip and twist in the air. Some say Siberians are like **acrobats**!

After playtime, Siberians are quiet and calm.

They chirp and purr to show love. Siberians make great family pets!

Glossary

acrobats—people who are good at doing tricks like jumping and balancing

breed—a type of cat

breeder—a person who purposely mates cats to make kittens with certain qualities

bushy—thick and full

coats—the hair or fur covering some animals

mousers—cats that catch mice

point coats—light-colored coats with darker fur in certain areas; pointed cats have dark faces, ears, legs, and tails.

ruffs—areas of longer fur around the necks of some animals

tabby—a pattern that has stripes, patches, or swirls of colors

tortoiseshell—a pattern of yellow, orange, and black with few or no patches of white

tufts—small bunches of long hair

To Learn More

AT THE LIBRARY

Brown, Domini. *Norwegian Forest Cats*. Minneapolis, Minn.: Bellwether Media, 2017.

Conley, Kate A. *Siberian Cats*. Minneapolis, Minn.: Checkerboard Animal Library, 2016.

Felix, Rebecca. *Maine Coons*. Minneapolis, Minn.: Bellwether Media, 2016.

ON THE WEB

Learning more about Siberian cats is as easy as 1, 2, 3.

1. Go to www.factsurfer.com.

2. Enter "Siberian cats" into the search box.

3. Click the "Surf" button and you will see a list of related web sites.

With factsurfer.com, finding more information is just a click away.

Index

The images in this book are reproduced through the courtesy of: Lubava, front cover; Zharinova Marina, p. 4; Petra Wegner/ Alamy, pp. 4-5, 11, 14-15; MaloriMay, pp. 6-7; Juniors Bildarchiv GmbH/ Alamy, p. 7; Tierfotoagentur/ Alamy, pp. 8-9, 12, 13, 17 (upper right, lower right), 20-21; imageBROKER/ Alamy, pp. 10-11; Kirill Vorobyev, p. 15; vvita, pp. 16-17; Alexander Korotun, p. 17 (upper left); SvetoGraf, p. 17 (lower left); GlobalP, p. 18; Massimo Cattaneo, pp. 18-19; Anna Utekhina, p. 21 (subject); Ingus Kruklitis, p. 21 (background).